FRANCISCO
PIZARRO

CONQUEROR OF THE INCAS

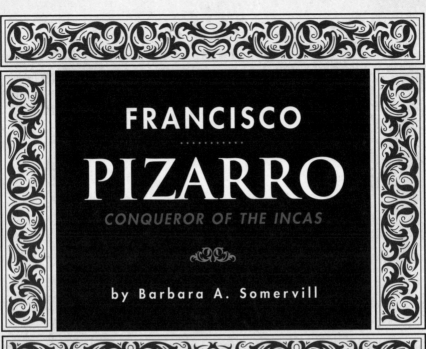

FRANCISCO
PIZARRO
CONQUEROR OF THE INCAS

by Barbara A. Somervill

Content Adviser: Sarah Chambers, Ph.D.,
Professor, Department of History,
University of Minnesota

Reading Adviser: Rosemary G. Palmer, Ph.D.,
Department of Literacy, College of Education,
Boise State University

COMPASS POINT BOOKS MINNEAPOLIS, MINNESOTA

Compass Point Books
3109 West 50th Street, #115
Minneapolis, MN 55410

Visit Compass Point Books on the Internet at *www.compassointbooks.com*
or e-mail your request to *custserv@compassointbooks.com.*

Editor: Jennifer VanVoorst
Lead Designer: Jaime Martens
Photo Researcher: Svetlana Zhurkina
Page Production: Heather Griffin
Cartographer: XNR Productions, Inc.
Educational Consultant: Diane Smolinski

Managing Editor: Catherine Neitge
Art Director: Keith Griffin
Production Director: Keith McCormick
Creative Director: Terri Foley

Library of Congress Cataloging-in-Publication Data
Somervill, Barbara A.
  Francisco Pizarro: conqueror of the Incas / by Barbara A. Somervill.
     p. cm. — (Signature lives)
  Includes bibliographical references and index.
  ISBN-13: 978-0-7565-0815-9 (hardcover)
  ISBN-10: 0-7565-0815-0 (hardcover)
  ISBN-13: 978-0-7565-1061-9 (paperback)
  ISBN-10: 0-7565-1061-9 (paperback)
  1. Pizarro, Francisco, ca. 1475–1541—Juvenile literature. 2. Peru—
History—Conquest, 1522–1548—Juvenile literature. 3. Conquerors—
Peru—Biography—Juvenile literature. 4. Conquerors—Spain—
Biography—Juvenile literature. 5. Explorers—Peru—Biography—Juvenile
literature. 6. Explorers—Spain—Biography—Juvenile literature. I. Title.
II. Series.
  F3442.P776S66 2004
  985'.02'092—dc22   2004017195

RENAISSANCE ERA

The Renaissance was a cultural movement that started in
Italy in the early 1300s. The word *renaissance* comes from
a Latin word meaning "rebirth," and during this time,
Europe experienced a rebirth of interest and achievement
in the arts, science, and global exploration. People reacted
against the religion-centered culture of the Middle Ages to
find greater value in the human world. By the time the
Renaissance came to a close, around 1600, people had come
to look at their world in a brand new way.

Table of Contents

1 GOLD FEVER

❧❧❧

Francisco Pizarro's eyes bulged with greed. Gold! Silver! Jewels beyond description! Francisco Pizarro had long burned to possess riches, and now he had the gold to feed his fever.

Pizarro and his small troop of Spanish soldiers camped in Cajamarca, a city in the Inca empire, now part of modern-day Peru. They had captured the Incas' ruler, Atahuallpa, and held him for ransom. Now, they waited for the king's ransom to arrive. The treasure they had demanded as ransom would make Pizarro and his men rich.

After weeks of waiting, Pizarro watched Inca nobles arrive in Cajamarca. Their caravans of servants and llamas stretched farther than the eye could see. Men and beasts carried the gold the Inca

The Inca culture created jewelry and decorative items of gold and other precious metals.

subjects believed would set their ruler free.

Pizarro ordered his secretary to record every bit of gold, silver, and gems the Incas delivered. There were beautiful gold and silver plates, carved with figures of the sun and moon. There were delicate bracelets, heavy gold necklaces, and armor made of beaten metal. The ransom room filled up with statues of Inca gods, deer, llamas, and birds. In footstools and benches, platters and pitchers, and goblets and bowls, the wealth of the Inca nation poured into Cajamarca.

Pizarro collected about 13,420 pounds (6,039 kilograms) of gold and 26,000 pounds (11,700 kg) of silver in all. But plates and stools and statues of llamas were awkward to divide. How many bracelets equaled one statue? Pizarro ordered the gold melted down and formed into gold coins. That made it easier to divide the treasure.

The king of Spain, of course, would get the largest portion, called the "royal fifth." Pizarro, the expedition leader, came next. But every officer and every soldier would get a share, and even a small fraction of the treasure provided wealth beyond imagining. The average cavalry soldier received 8,880 gold pieces and 362 silver marcs. This would be roughly 94 pounds (43 kg) of gold and 180 pounds (82 kg) of silver. At today's prices, a soldier's share would be worth nearly $1.3 million and Pizarro's portion was six times as large!

A statue of Francisco Pizarro stands in a public square in his hometown of Trujillo, Spain.

With the ransom paid, Pizarro's thoughts turned to one last problem. He knew that when Atahuallpa was freed, the Inca army would attack the Spaniards. His small force would be no match against the full strength of the Inca army. How could he make sure he didn't lose his treasure? After waiting a lifetime for this wealth, Pizarro wasn't about to give up even

11 ➷

a single gold piece. He decided that Atahuallpa had to die. And so Atahuallpa found himself on trial for his life. The verdict was already decided. The Inca ruler was guilty and would be executed.

Today, historians look back on Pizarro's conquests with amazement. Fewer than 200 soldiers had marched into the heart of the Inca empire and brought it to its knees. They defeated an army of thousands and conquered an empire of millions.

Francisco Pizarro, an ignorant soldier who couldn't read or write, planned an ambush and captured a king. He filled his pockets with Inca gold. He established Spanish cities in the New World and became governor of the territory that is present-day Peru. The gold he sent back to his country helped Spain become the greatest power in Europe for most of the 15th and 16th centuries.

But Pizarro was hated by the Inca natives and envied by his peers. He snuffed out an empire that had thrived for hundreds of years and forever changed a people whose history went back even further. Pizarro died in a pool of his own blood,

Gold Pizarro took from the Incas was used to fund wars in Europe, as well as to create items such as this altar in a Panama cathedral.

attacked by fellow Spaniards. He left behind a legacy of greed and destruction as Spain and its conquistadors brought colonial rule to the South American continent. ✎

2 EARLY LIFE

Chapter

⤳⟨✕⟩⤲

In the late 1400s, Pizarro's hometown of Trujillo, Spain, was already a very old city, with a history stretching back more than 2,000 years. Trujillo was a typical medieval fortress, built on a hilltop with tall granite walls to protect the city. Inside the walls were plazas, churches, and palaces. Behind the city center, however, lay a web of streets with hundreds of small, dark homes. Open sewers ran through city streets. People emptied human waste from chamber pots into the gutters. Rats crawled through open garbage in search of scraps to eat. Flies laid live maggots on bones with rotting meat.

Because of these unsanitary conditions, diseases flourished. Few medicines existed, and antibiotics would not be invented for another 500 years.

Trujillo is in the Extremadura province of Spain, which was the poorest area of the country in Pizarro's time.

Smallpox, measles, whooping cough, flu, and plague ran through Spain as they did through other European countries. Families expected several of their children to die before the age of 5. If half a family's children lived to adulthood, that family was lucky.

It was into this environment that Francisco Pizarro was born. It was common to record births, deaths, and marriages in a church, court, or family Bible, but no record of Francisco's birth has been found. His actual birth date remains a mystery, although historians believe he was born sometime between 1471 and 1475.

Some historians claim that Francisco was abandoned as an infant on the steps of a local church. Others claim that he was raised with swine and nursed by a sow—a rather bizarre rumor. In reality, Pizarro's father, Colonel Gonzalo Pizarro, was an army officer. His soldiers called him "the Roman" because of his feats against the Italians, and "the Tall" because of his height. Pizarro's mother, Francisca Gonzalez, worked as a servant. Although his parents never married, Pizarro's mother and father each produced a number of half brothers for Francisco.

Pizarro's hometown of Trujillo was located in a province of Spain called Extremadura. The province's name means "remote and harsh" in Latin. Extremadura was the poorest area of the country. This province was also home to Hernán Cortés, who conquered the Aztec empire of modern-day Mexico.

Neither parent showed much interest in Francisco. Young Francisco never went to school, and he never learned to read or write. Not many children attended school at that time. Instead, Francisco began working early in life. His first job was as a swineherd. Raising pigs was a filthy job, but it was no disgrace. Many boys from Pizarro's home province of Extremadura found work as swine-herds. The job provided money for food and clothing. However, the work was dreary, and Francisco Pizarro had big dreams. He wanted adventure, excitement, and, most importantly, great wealth.

No portrait of Pizarro that exists today was painted during his lifetime. All were painted based on descriptions of what he looked like.

As a teenager, Pizarro joined the army, which may have been his only way to escape poverty. Army life may have been demanding, but it provided cloth-ing, daily food, and some amount of money.

At that time, Spanish forces were engaged in an ongoing battle with the Moors, an Islamic people from the kingdom of Granada in what is now south-ern Spain. The Spanish monarchs, Ferdinand and

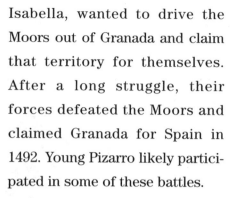

When Pizarro was born, Spain was made up of several smaller kingdoms. In 1469, a marriage united the kingdoms of Castile and Aragon. Later wars and conquests added the kingdoms of Granada and Navarre to make up the territory of present-day Spain.

Isabella, wanted to drive the Moors out of Granada and claim that territory for themselves. After a long struggle, their forces defeated the Moors and claimed Granada for Spain in 1492. Young Pizarro likely participated in some of these battles.

In 1492, Spain's King Ferdinand and Queen Isabella had many expenses. They paid for and supplied an army to protect them from invasion by other European countries. They maintained many castles and servants. Dukes, dons, and their families visited court for months on end, and the royal family paid for their guests' food and housing. The royals needed a quick route to the great wealth found in China and the Spice Islands.

Christopher Columbus, an Italian, proposed a plan to sail west toward these eastern lands. He wanted to claim their spices, gems, and precious metals for Spain. King Ferdinand and Queen Isabella paid Christopher Columbus's travel expenses to find such a route.

Although educated people at that time knew that the world was round, they recognized that Columbus risked great danger. Many believed

Columbus had miscalculated the distance he would need to travel to reach Asia. Although he didn't find a sea route to Asia, Columbus did find land—probably what we know today as the Bahamas. When he returned, he shared news of a "New World" that excited the Spanish royal court.

Columbus did not return with great treasure, but he brought back unfamiliar food and crops, such as corn, potatoes, and tobacco, as well as parrots and

In 1492, Spain's king and queen sent explorer Christopher Columbus on a voyage to find a western sea route to the lands known as the Indies. Young Pizarro dreamed of such adventure.

In the 15th and 16th centuries, Spain and Portugal were in a race to find a route to China, the Spice Islands, and the other lands known as the Indies. But while the Spanish headed westward and established colonies in the Americas, Portuguese explorers mainly sailed south down the coast of Africa and settled colonies on that continent. In 1498, the Portuguese explorer Vasco de Gama sailed around the southern tip of Africa and reached India.

seven natives he had captured. Columbus also presented the royals with a few small samples of gold and pearls, and he promised much more could be taken from the lands he had found. Soon, all of Spain buzzed with news of riches beyond the western sea. Every explorer wanted to go to this strange place and become rich.

Among the would-be fortune hunters was the young soldier Francisco Pizarro, who was now about 20 years old. When he heard about this new land and its promise of great wealth, he itched to seek his own fortune in this new western world.

In 1502, Pizarro got his chance. He traveled to Seville in southern Spain. There, he caught a ship to the island of Hispaniola, along with the colony's new governor. Columbus had established the first European settlement on the island in 1493, and by the early 1500s, the island served as the first Spanish outpost in the heart of the Caribbean Sea. Today, the countries of Haiti and the Dominican Republic occupy the island.

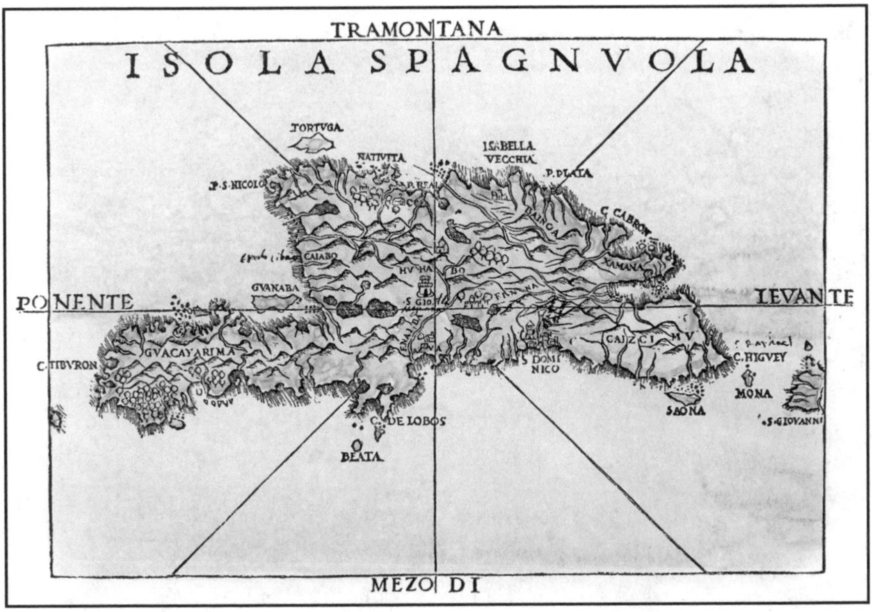

This map of the island of Hispaniola was made in 1534. By this time, the island had many settlements.

Now about 30 years old, Pizarro became a member of the governor's military troops in Hispaniola and served in that post for several years.

Few could have imagined that this inexperienced, uneducated soldier would gain riches as a conquistador in the New World. But for Pizarro, dreams of wealth and power burned strong and deep.

3 Chapter
In The New World

For many, the island of Hispaniola was the starting point for further exploration in the lands Columbus had termed the "New World." For several years, Francisco Pizarro yearned to join expeditions departing Hispaniola to explore the New World. Although he served his governor well by protecting the Spanish colonies from hostile natives, every expedition stirred dreams of wealth in Pizarro. His chance finally came. Pizarro joined Alonzo de Ojeda on an expedition to present-day Colombia and Venezuela.

Few explorers could afford to pay their soldiers. Instead, a share of the treasure replaced their wages. As an officer, Pizarro would receive a large share of whatever items the expedition collected.

In 1513, Spanish explorer Vasco Nuñez de Balboa was the first European to see the Pacific Ocean. Pizarro was a member of Balboa's expedition.

Although the colonists left San Sebastian to return to Hispaniola in the early 1500s, the colony survived. This illustration of San Sebastian was made at the end of the 16th century.

Unfortunately for Pizarro, Ojeda made poor choices, and his men suffered dearly. In 1509, Ojeda and his company set up the colony of San Sebastian in a low-lying, swampy region of present-day northern Colombia. The colony quickly ran short of food. His men endured swarms of mosquitoes, fevers, and diarrhea. Hostile natives regularly shot at them with arrows dipped in poison. The colony's location offered no gold, silver, or gems. It barely supported the colonists who suffered through months of torment.

Ojeda left San Sebastian to return to Hispaniola. He planned to load up on supplies and weapons, and add new soldiers to protect his colony. He left Francisco Pizarro in charge of San Sebastian. While Ojeda was gone, the colony lost many to hunger, disease, and poisoned arrows. The colonists who survived finally gave up. With their numbers now small enough to fit onto the two remaining ships, the colonists abandoned San Sebastian to return to Hispaniola.

Pizarro took advantage of the opportunity and made a hasty departure. He headed for Cartagena, in present-day northern Colombia, and left his loyalty to Ojeda behind him. Since there had been no treasure, he had received no payment.

In Cartagena, Pizarro joined another company of explorers, led by Martín Fernandez de Enciso. Accompanying them was a stowaway named Vasco Nuñez de Balboa. Enciso's new company, including Pizarro and Balboa, settled the colony of Santa Maria de Antiqua del Darién, in modern-day Panama. This settlement was just across the Gulf of Urabá from where San Sebastian had failed. Enciso placed Balboa in charge of the colony and headed off in search of bigger rewards.

Natives had told Balboa of a great sea and land of gold that lay to the south. In 1513, Balboa organized a company to search for this land, and Pizarro became its captain. Marching westward through

> *Vasco Nuñez de Balboa was from Pizarro's home province of Extremadura, Spain. He came to the New World to be a farmer. He was not successful and was continually troubled by debt. In order to avoid his creditors, he became a stowaway on Enciso's ship.*

the interior of Panama, 190 Spaniards and hundreds of natives hacked through steaming jungles thick with vines and strangler figs. In their heavy clothes and armor, the Spanish all but cooked themselves in the heat. Day and night, mosquitoes, gnats, and other insects plagued the explorers.

When they slashed through the last bit of dense jungle, they came upon a massive body of water. Balboa stepped into the waves and said, "Long live

Balboa claimed the Pacific Ocean for Spain.

the mighty and powerful kings of Castile! In their name, I take possession of these seas and regions." Balboa named the sea *El Mar del Sur,* or the Southern Sea. Today, it is called the Pacific Ocean. While this ocean may have been spectacular, it was not gold. And Pizarro remained true to his primary goal of getting rich by any means.

Seeking a new chance at wealth, Pizarro left Balboa's men and joined the troops of the new governor of Panama, Pedrarias Dávila. Pedrarias sent Pizarro and another officer named Morales to raid the tribes of Panama's Pacific Coast. They robbed villages on nearby islands, stealing gold, silver, and pearls, along with whatever jewels they could find.

Pedrarias rewarded Pizarro and Morales for their efforts. They received a portion of the spoils and land near the newly founded capital city of Panama. Pizarro had finally reached the status of landed gentleman. He had a handful of gold and gems and a large plot of swampland too unhealthy to support a house or raise crops.

Although Balboa left Panama on further explorations, the ambitious Governor Pedrarias still thought of Balboa as a rival for power. In 1519, Pedrarias ordered Pizarro to arrest Vasco Nuñez de Balboa for treason, theft from the Spanish king, and poor treatment of native people. To make the arrest, Pedrarias needed to separate Balboa from his loyal

Map shows modern boundaries.

Gulf of Mexico

Atlantic Ocean

Cuba

Hispaniola

Jamaica

0   400 miles
0   400 kilometers

Pacific Ocean

Cartagena

Panama City   Acla

San Sebastian

PANAMA   *Puerto de Piñas*   Santa Maria de Antigua del Darien

Punta Quemada

San Juan River

NORTH AMERICA

SOUTH AMERICA

Isla de Gallo

COLOMBIA

N W E S

In the early 1500s, Pizarro explored the New World as a member of various expeditions.

troops. He sent Balboa a letter asking for a private meeting in the city of Acla.

The messenger was suspicious of Pedrarias's motives and warned Balboa that his life was in danger. Balboa planned to marry Pedrarias's daughter. He could not believe that his future father-in-law would betray him. So, Balboa continued on to Acla.

On the way, Balboa's group met Pizarro and the

armed company sent to arrest Balboa. Pizarro and Balboa had been friends for some time. They had traveled together and been the first Europeans to see the Pacific Ocean. Balboa was confused and exclaimed, "What is this, Francisco Pizarro? How is it possible that you have come in this way to receive me!" Pizarro's men took Balboa into custody. They escorted him to Acla and placed him under guard.

Balboa's trial followed shortly. Although Balboa pleaded innocent, the verdict had already been determined. He was found guilty and sentenced to death. To make sure that the Spanish king would not pardon Balboa, Pedrarias ordered that the execution take place immediately.

Balboa climbed the scaffold. He declared,

> *It is a lie and falsehood which is charged against me! Never did I entertain such a thought. It was always my intention to serve the King as a faithful and loyal vassal, and my desire to enlarge his domains with all my power and strength.*

His protests fell on deaf ears. Balboa placed his head on the block and was quickly beheaded. For his role in capturing Balboa, Pizarro earned the sincere appreciation of Pedrarias Dávila. ✒

4 In Search of Birú

Chapter

After Balboa's death, Pizarro retired as a soldier and lived on the land he had been given. He served as mayor and judge of a newly founded town. However, news of other Spaniards' conquests kept his dreams of wealth alive.

In 1521, the great Aztec empire of modern-day Mexico fell to conquistador Hernán Cortés. All of Spain buzzed with talk of the massive wealth Cortés collected raiding Aztec palaces and temples. The brutality, cruelty, and violence shown by Cortés's army toward the Aztecs were brushed aside. Cortés shipped boatloads of gold, silver, and gems to Spain. The news of such magnificent riches gave Pizarro's greed new life. Surely, if Cortés found such wealth, so could Pizarro.

Natives, seeing the Spaniards' interest in gold, told them of a wealthy land to the south called Birú.

In the taverns and inns of Panama, Pizarro heard rumors of a great empire to the south, called Birú, now present-day Peru. There, he was certain, masses of gold and gems could be found. Pizarro was nearly 50 years old, already an old man in those days, and he feared time was running out for him to become rich. He would join an expedition to the South. He would at last find his own gold.

In 1522, Pizarro joined a company heading south along Panama's Pacific Coast. However, shortly after embarking, the leader got sick, and the expedition ended almost as soon as it had begun. It was not a total loss, though, because while on the expedition, Pizarro became close friends with Diego de Almagro. They shared much in common. The two men were about the same age, and neither could read nor write. Both men survived poverty as children and wanted great wealth as adults.

Pizarro and Almagro could not afford to launch an expedition on their own, so they joined forces. Hernando de Luque, a Roman Catholic priest, served as a middleman between the explorers and Spaniards with money. Each partner had a different function in the expedition. Pizarro would lead the men on the venture. Almagro became quartermaster, collecting needed supplies, food, and weapons, and signing up about 100 men. Luque paid the bills and got whatever official approvals were needed.

Diego de Almagro joined Pizarro on many expeditions.

The men accompanying Pizarro and Almagro were a scruffy bunch. Most signed up because they had little money or to avoid being put in jail. They had some military background, but were mostly stragglers rather than soldiers.

Luque and Almagro purchased two small ships

from the fleet standing idle in Panama City harbor. Oddly, the larger of the two ships had been built by Balboa, who before his death had planned a similar expedition south. With everything at the ready, Pizarro and Almagro weighed anchor in November 1524—the worst possible season for travel in that region.

Rain poured down day after day. Wind whipped the Pacific Ocean and bounced the small ships around like corks in a stream. Almagro, sensing that

In the 1500s, sailors used small ships called caravels to explore rivers and coastlines.

supplies would run short, headed home to Panama to restock.

Pizarro escaped the open ocean at a place called *Puerto de Pinas*, or Port of Pines. He turned his ship to sail up the River Birú and dropped anchor. His military troops left the ship to explore the countryside. Pizarro's men found coastal land to the south sodden and swampy, much like Panama and Colombia. Pools of still water lay under a blanket of green algae and buzzed with insects. The muck underfoot made marching difficult for the soldiers. The weapons they carried only added to their burdens as the company trudged through hilly countryside.

Pizarro's men roasted in the heat in thick cotton or wool doublets under a vest of chain mail, a fabric made of steel rings that could protect them from stone or metal-tipped spears. They carried daggers, swords, muskets, and crossbows, prepared for attacks from natives.

The troops marched farther inland over rocky paths. Many of the men cut their feet through their thin, worn boots. Everyone bore the itchy bites of swarming mosquitoes. The men returned to their ship having found nothing worth taking. They did not even find fruit, game birds, or fish worth catching. Pizarro did not worry. He was certain that riches lay to the south, and that the expedition simply had not traveled far enough.

Almost as soon as Pizarro put to sea again, a huge storm arose. Waves surged and broke over the ship. For nearly 10 days, the damaging storm raged while Pizarro's men clung to solid posts and railings. The company ate little, but food rations still became scarce. They needed fresh water and meat. By the time the storm ended, the men were surviving on two ears of dried corn per day.

They approached a small island with dense jungle growing right to the edge. The men, near starvation, wanted desperately to return to Panama. Pizarro would not hear of such a thing. The soldiers, weakend by hunger, hacked their way through thick

This Spanish soldier of the 1500s aims a gun called an arquebus.

shrubs. They ate berries, many of which proved poisonous. Those who did not die suffered crippling stomach cramps. Some men resorted to eating raw crabs and shellfish.

Weeks passed with still no sign of Almagro's supply ship. Pizarro and his men headed farther inland where they found a native village. The Spaniards rushed in and took corn and coconuts from the native huts. The owners of the food were too surprised to act. Pizarro noticed that many of the natives wore gold jewelry. The design and workmanship was crude, but Pizarro did not want gold for decoration. He wanted to be wealthy. More than ever before, he believed that wealth lay beyond the horizon.

Six weeks later, the supply ship sent by Almagro finally arrived. The ship's captain barely recognized Pizarro and his men. Many had starved to death, and those who remained were filthy, worn out, and wasted from hunger. Finally fed and supplied, Pizarro and his remaining company bid farewell to the place the Spaniards came to call *Puerto de la Hambre*—Hunger Port.

Pizarro again turned his ships south to continue his search for Birú. They anchored off the coast near what looked to be a quiet native village. The Spaniards were in for a nasty surprise. They found the village deserted, but managed to find small stores of dried corn and other food items.

The Caribs were an aggressive group of native tribes who frequently waged war. According to some accounts, they would kill and eat any enemies they captured in battle. The English word cannibal comes from the Spanish name for these tribes.

Some gold jewelry was discovered in huts. But shock set in when the Spaniards investigated the campfires. They found the remains of roasted human flesh. They had come upon one of the few tribes of cannibals in the Caribbean and tropical Pacific, the Caribs. The Spanish made a hasty retreat. They had no desire to become dinner for the Caribs.

Farther south, Pizarro came to a place he named *Punta Quemada*, or Burned Point. Thick mangrove swamps lined the shore. After much effort to cut through the tangled root network, the Spaniards came upon a large, prosperous native village. At first, the natives ran away, shocked by the sight of the bearded, armored Spaniards. Pizarro's company lost no time in searching the huts for food and valuables. They came away with plenty of food and a small amount of gold.

The natives were not the cowards the Spanish imagined them to be. They had moved into the jungle to keep an eye on the Spanish. They hid their women and children deep in the tropical forest. When Pizarro sent part of the company inland to investigate the area, the natives attacked. The Spanish countered the attack with crossbows and guns. Although the Spanish won, several soldiers died and more suffered wounds in the skirmish.

Pizarro retreated to yet another island not far from Panama. His men were hungry, weary, and needed time to heal. His ship had been damaged by heavy storms. Pizarro decided to remain on the island while a group took his ship back to Panama for repairs.

Back in Panama, Almagro had fitted out another ship and prepared to follow Pizarro's trail. He planned to find his partner by locating places where Pizarro had stopped and left hatchet marks on coastal trees. Unfortunately for Almagro, he made it to Punta Quemada where the warrior natives were still enraged over their meeting with Pizarro.

On land, the Spanish conquistadors often traveled on horseback. They sometimes used natives to carry their belongings.

When Almagro landed, he met the same violence as Pizarro. Foolishly, Almagro lost his temper and attacked instead of retreating. He burned native homes and ordered his men forward. In the battle that followed, Almagro received a spear wound to the head. The infection that followed cost Almagro the sight in one eye. Despite this, Almagro continued his journey, stopping at small villages and robbing the natives along the way.

After accumulating a cargo of gold, Almagro headed back to Panama. On the way, he discovered that Pizarro was camped on a nearby island. Almagro collected Pizarro and his company, and they all returned to Panama far richer than when they had left. It was not enough gold from Pizarro's viewpoint, but it was a good start.

Two years later, the partners made yet another attempt to find Birú. In November 1526, they left Panama with 160 men, two ships, and several horses. After a slow start, Almagro returned to Panama for supplies. Pizarro camped by the San Juan River with his men. Their ship's pilot Ruiz continued sailing along the river.

Ruiz's ship met a raft heading northward. The raft carried 20 native people and their goods for trading. It was a large wooden raft with a large cotton sail. The Spanish found jewelry, cloth, and other goods of great value. There were belts, bracelets, necklaces, and pins made of gold, silver, and gems. The traders carried ornate silver mirrors, cups, and plates. They had finely woven wools and cottons, and many cloth items had been embroidered with birds, flowers, and animals. The Spanish wanted to know where the goods came from. The answer was what they had expected all along—from a wealthy land to the south.

These items— a gold figure with outstreched arms and an embroidered poncho— come from the Inca culture of present-day Peru.

While waiting for Almagro to return, Pizarro made a serious mistake. He moved his men to Isla de Gallo, an island in a swamp just north of the equator. Mosquitoes swarmed day and night, biting the men. The troops became sick and several men died every week. The men grew angry after months of hardship and were ready to mutiny.

Soon, however, two ships arrived. Instead of sending supplies, the governor of Panama had sent ships to the island, and he enouraged Pizarro to give up his expedition and return to Panama. Pizarro's men were overjoyed. Pedro de Cieza de Leon, a chronicler of the Spanish conquest of Peru, recorded the tale as told to him by one of Pizarro's soldiers:

> *Pizarro was downcast when he saw they all wanted to go. He quietly composed himself and said that, of course, they could return to Panama and the choice was theirs. He had not wanted them to leave because they would have their reward if and when they discovered a good land. As for himself, he felt that returning poor to Panama was a harder thing than staying to face death and hardship.*

Pizarro had nutured his dream of wealth too long to give up now. He drew a line in the sand with his sword. He said,

Friends and comrades! On that side [south] are toil, hunger, nakedness, the drenching storm, desertion, and death; on this side ease and pleasure. There lies Peru with its riches; here, Panama and its poverty. Choose, each man, what best becomes a brave Castilian [Spaniard]. For my part, I go to the south.

Faced with continued hardships, Pizarro drew a line in the sand and challenged his men to cross it.

Although most members of the expedition chose to return to Panama, 13 men crossed the line to join Pizarro.

43

5 THE INCA EMPIRE

⟨✦⟩

The Spanish conquistadors were in search of a city of gold. What they found was the Inca empire. The vast Inca empire ran roughly 3,400 miles (5,440 kilometers) north to south along the Andes Mountains. It covered the dry desert land along the coast of the Pacific Ocean to the Amazon rain forests on the Andes's eastern slopes. Parts of modern-day Ecuador, Colombia, Brazil, Argentina, Bolivia, and Chile, and all of present-day Peru once belonged to the Inca empire.

The Inca called their empire Tahuanitinsuyu, which meant "Land of the Four Quarters." More than 10 million people lived within the four quarters. Nearly 15,000 miles (24,000 km) of paved roads connected Inca cities to Cuzco, the capital. Along each

The Incas worshipped the sun god, Inti. They built temples and held festivals in his honor.

Although the Incas did not have a written language, they used a device called a quipu to send messages. A quipu was a thick cord from which hung strings of various colors and lengths. Information was represented by the length of the cord, the color and position of string, and the type and position of the knots. Only skilled people could interpret quipus.

road travelers found *tambos*, small storehouses with grain, dried meat, and blankets. Travelers ate and rested there on their long journeys. A string of messengers ran in short shifts from tambo to tambo carrying messages for government officials and the Inca army.

The Inca government was a model of organization. At the top was the Sapa Inca, or great chief. The word *Inca* means "chief" and at one time referred only to the ruler. When the word later came to refer to the civilization as a whole, the ruler became known as the Sapa Inca. The people believed that the Sapa Inca was the "son of the Sun," or the child of their main god. The Sapa Inca himself was revered and honored as a god, and his orders were followed without question.

Supporting the Sapa Inca were nobles in charge of neatly divided regions. The Incas divided their empire into four main regions. Each had a noble leader or governor who reported back to the Sapa Inca. Further divisions broke down the population into groups of 10,000, 5,000, 1,000, 500, 100, 50, and

DEPOCITODELINGA
COLLCA

topaynga yupanqui

An Inca official delivers a report to a nobleman using a quipu.

10 families. Each group of 10 families had a leader who reported to the leader of 50 families, and so on up the line.

Common Inca subjects lived very simple lives. They followed these simple rules: Do not be lazy, steal, lie, commit adultery, or murder. Incas knew what their lives would be like. They worked hard, paid taxes, and wanted for nothing. The government ensured they would have fields to farm, a home to live in, and food if they were hungry.

Inca people were born into their professions. A child of a farmer would become a farmer. The child of an artist would become an artist. The government leaders monitored all work and group production.

Nearly every Inca commoner farmed and produced food and clothing.

Every family unit paid tax, but the tax was paid in labor. One-third of all their labor was spent working the lands of the Sapa Inca. Crops from the Sapa Inca's land were stored for later use, usually when crops failed. They gave another third of their time to the priests and temples. Food from the temples' fields fed the people at religious festivals. They spent the final third of their time working their own land.

The Sapa Inca was commander in chief of the military. Supporting him were generals, captains, lieutenants, and many soldiers. Without orders from the Sapa Inca, the Inca army would not act.

While Pizarro wallowed in swamp water, major changes took place among the Incas. In 1524, an epidemic—most likely smallpox—swept through South America. This deadly disease was introduced to the region by Spanish explorers who visited South America before Pizarro. Since the Incas had never been exposed to the disease before, they had not developed immunity and therefore died in great numbers. The Sapa Inca Huayna Capac contracted the disease

During the 1400s, the Inca empire expanded as warrior chiefs conquered neighboring civilizations. The conquered people were largely allowed to maintain their own cultures. Nevertheless, the Incas mixed with the conquered peoples. Of the 10 million people in the Inca empire, only about 40,000 were of purely Inca descent.

sometime between 1525 and 1527.

An Inca chronicler, Garcilaso Inca de la Vega, recorded Huayna Capac's death as told to him by a witness. Vega wrote that, as he lay on his deathbed, Huayna Capac told his attendants,

> *Our Father the Sun has revealed to me that after the reign of twelve Incas, his own children, there will appear in our country an unknown race of men who will subdue our Empire. ... The reign of the twelve Incas ends with me. I can therefore certify to you that these people will return shortly after I have left you, and that they will accomplish what our Father the Sun predicted they would.*

After delivering this bad news, Huayna Capac named his son Ninan Cuyusi as the next Sapa Inca. It was a tradition among Inca rulers that they choose the next to lead. Unfortunately, Huayna Capac chose an infant son who died within days of his father. This left the empire without a ruler.

Many Incas believed that Huáscar, another son of Huayna Capac, was the next rightful leader. Huáscar took control of the throne and the Inca capital city of Cuzco. However, before his death Huayna Capac had divided his empire and his army, declaring Quito as a second capital. In the Quito region, Atahuallpa, another son, declared himself heir to the throne and embarked on a civil war.

Timing played a major role in Pizarro's success as a conquistador. While Atahuallpa and Huáscar battled, Almagro arrived at Pizarro's camp with food, supplies, and more men. The expedition and some local natives began to sail down the west coast of South America. In the distance, the Andes Mountains rose high against the sky.

In 1528, Pizarro landed in Tumbes, an active seaport on present-day Peru's northwest border. The natives welcomed the odd-looking foreigners to their city. The natives found the Spaniards strange because they grew hair on their faces, which native men could not do. The Spanish custom of covering their bodies from head to toe in clothing amused the Inca people. They could not imagine wearing so much clothing in such heat.

The Spanish found Tumbes remarkable. Solidly built stone temples rose beside a broad city square. Plates and statues of gold and silver decorated the temples. Tidy homes spread out along orderly, paved streets. Tumbes was clean, healthy, and free of crime. It did not have stinking open sewers or garbage lining the streets like Spanish cities of the time.

The Incas built their stone temples without using any mortar. Nevertheless, many of these buildings are still standing today. They have withstood not only time, but also the earthquakes that sometimes shake the area.

Tumbes's governor provided food and fresh water for Pizarro's ship. The governor invited Francisco Pizarro to eat with him. The Inca governor asked where the strangers had come from, and Pizarro explained through interpreters that they came from a great country called Spain. Pizarro told of the power of their king, Charles V, and of the Spaniards' one true God. Pizarro's comments shocked the Incas, who believed in several gods, including Inti, the all-powerful sun god.

Now that the Spaniards knew where to find Birú, they needed permission from the Spanish king to conquer the Inca empire. In late 1528, Pizarro returned to Spain to seek royal approval for himself, Almagro, and Luque to embark on such a venture. At the court in Toledo, Spain, Pizarro described the lands, people, and wealth of the Inca empire. He showed the king and queen items he had brought from the New World: gold, jewels, embroidered cloths, llama fleece, and a newly drawn map of Peru. The king and queen paid careful attention to Pizarro's tales. Perhaps their greatest interest lay in the promise of wealth.

In July 1529, the queen of Spain signed a charter allowing Pizarro to invade the Incas. Pizarro was named governor and captain of all conquests in Peru, or New Castile, as the Spanish now called the land. Spain's king and queen also made Pizarro a

knight of the Order of Santiago, Spain's highest order of knighthood, with the right to have a coat of arms. Almagro became commandant of Tumbes. Luque received the title Protector of the Indians and would eventually become the bishop of Tumbes.

Pizarro sought and gained approval from Charles V of Spain to invade the Incas.

In January 1530, Pizarro prepared to sail westward to Panama with the royal charter firmly in his grasp. He brought with him his half brothers Hernando, Juan, and Gonzalo Pizarro, and another half brother Francisco Martinez de Alcántara. Pedro Pizarro, a 15-year-old cousin, joined the expedition as a servant. He later wrote an account of the voyage and conquest.

Upon his return to Panama, Francisco Pizarro entered into yet another contract with Almagro. Nearly a year later, three ships left Panama City under the leadership of Francisco Pizarro. The company was made up of 180 men—including his four half brothers—and a number of horses, guns, and crossbows. A young conquistador named Hernando de Soto later arrived with reinforcements.

Although they frequently quarrelled, Pizarro, Almagro, and Luque renewed their contract for another expedition.

The expedition arrived in Tumbes to discover that the Inca civil war had left that city in ruins. While the state of Tumbes must have disappointed

Almagro and Luque, it encouraged Francisco Pizarro. A war would allow Pizarro to venture deep into the empire without being disturbed. With a bit of trickery on Pizarro's part, the Spanish might just defeat the warring Incas.

Despite the civil war, most of the Inca empire remained intact. Some cities suffered ruin, while others seemed to prosper. For the average Inca citizen, the war's outcome had little impact. Ultimately, one ruler was not much different from another.

Atahuallpa proved to be the better military leader and won the war. He took the throne and declared himself Sapa Inca. He arranged for Huáscar to be captured and held in prison. Atahuallpa knew he would be accused of stealing the title and wanted to protect himself from a revolution by the other Inca nobles. Atahuallpa prevented action by Huáscar's close relatives by killing nearly 1,000 of Huáscar's supporters. With a firm grip on the empire, Atahuallpa and his army proceeded to Cajamarca, a city in the heart of the Andes Mountains.

Messengers arrived to tell the new Sapa Inca of strangers traveling in the empire:

> *The messengers ... told the Inca how some strange people never seen before who preached new doctrines and laws had*

landed on the beach. These men were so bold that they did not fear dangerous things; they were stuffed into their clothes which covered them head to foot; they were white and had beards and a ferocious appearance.

Atahuallpa sent gifts to the strangers. He gave permission for them to travel through the Inca empire and showed little concern about this handful of men.

Pizarro's company traveled along the paved Inca roadway, heading toward, they hoped, an abundance of gold. The moist jungle air became cold and dry. The company and their horses struggled on the steep and narrow mountain roads. Sheer rock walls rose up on one side of the road and dropped away on the other, revealing a steep drop to the valley below. Had the Sapa Inca wanted to stop the advance of Pizarro's forces, a small army could easily have done so.

While the Sapa Inca and his army in Cajamarca waited for Pizarro to arrive, they sent mes-

The Andes are the world's longest chain of mountains. They continue north to south for 4,500 miles (7,200 kilometers), and span 400 miles (640 km) at their widest. The Andes are also the second-highest mountain range in the world, after the Himalayas. Many of the Andes mountains are active volcanoes. The name comes from the word anti, which means copper in the Inca language of Quechua. Copper, as well as gold, silver, and other precious metals, has been found in the Andes Mountains.

Maximum extent of Inca empire, 1493–1525

Map shows modern boundaries.

COLOMBIA

Quito

ECUADOR

Tumbes

BRAZIL

Cajamarca

PERU

Ciudad de los Reyes (Lima)

Rímac River

Vilcabamba

Cuzco

Lake Titicaca

BOLIVIA

Pacific Ocean

N W E S

0   400 miles

0   400 kilometers

CHILE

PARAGUAY

ARGENTINA

NORTH AMERICA

SOUTH AMERICA

Andes Mountains

sengers to assure the Spaniards of their peaceful intentions. Though Pizarro, too, offered friendship to the Incas, he had conquest on his mind. ✍

The Inca empire covered nearly 3,400 miles (5,440 km) along the Andes.

6 MASSACRE IN CAJAMARCA

Chapter

ややや

In 1532, Pizarro's troops arrived in Cajamarca. This large town featured well-built stone and adobe buildings. A palace and a temple stood on a broad plaza. About 30,000 Inca soldiers camped on a hillside above the town. This was the camp of the Sapa Inca, Atahuallpa.

Pizarro's company approached the Inca king. Spanish armor gleamed in the bright sun. Many soldiers rode horseback, astonishing the Incas, who had never seen horses before. They shot guns that roared like thunder. Trumpets blared and horses snorted.

Atahuallpa sat under a tent decorated with fine cloth and gold. Inca elders who wore huge gold earrings stayed behind their leader. A bodyguard of 400 warriors stood by Atahuallpa's side. Francisco

As part of a plan to trap and attack the Sapa Inca and his followers, the Spanish priest urged Atahuallpa to accept Christianity.

Pizarro showed no fear. He rode up to the king and invited him to dinner.

Pizarro waited several days for Atahuallpa to show up. When the king finally came, it was in full splendor. Hundreds of servants, all dressed in red and white, walked ahead of their ruler. They cleared the road so that Atahuallpa's litter could proceed without jarring the Sapa Inca. Musicians played flutes, drums, and conch-shell trumpets. Dancers swayed to the rhythms of the Inca chants. A gold and silver litter appeared, carried by 80 powerful men. Fans and shades made of red, blue, and green feathers protected Atahuallpa from the sun's heat. The ruler himself appeared in clothes covered with gold and gems. He wore the traditional red woven crown of the Sapa Inca and a tunic woven with gold threads. He carried a gold staff and wore gold sandals on his feet.

A Spanish priest, Fray Vicente Valverde, stepped forward to read from the Bible. He urged Atahuallpa to accept Christianity and the Spanish king. Francisco de Xeres, Pizarro's secretary, recorded the priest's words:

> *I am a priest of God, and I teach Christians the things of God, and in like manner I come to teach you. What I teach is that which God says to us in this Book. Therefore, on the part of God and of the*

Christians, I beseech you to be their friend, for such is God's will, and it will be for your good.

Atahuallpa demanded to see the Bible. The Incas had no written language and could neither read nor write. To Atahuallpa, the book was useless. He asked, "Why does the Book not say anything to me?" He threw it to the ground in disgust, insulting the Spaniards.

Pizarro's plan from the beginning had been to ambush Atahuallpa. So few Spaniards could not possibly defeat Atahuallpa's 30,000 warriors. Pizarro's dinner invitation was a trick to help him

Pizarro and his men planned their attack so that they would be fighting only a small number of Atahuallpa's soldiers.

separate the king from his army. When Atahuallpa threw the Bible aside, Pizarro ordered the attack.

Pizarro had prepared well for Atahuallpa's arrival. He had chosen a section of the town that was surrounded on three sides by buildings. Pizarro had hidden most of his men and their horses in those buildings.

When the attack began, the noise was tremendous, and the Incas were thrown into a panic. Trumpets blared and guns boomed. The Spanish soldiers hacked through the guards and elders with swords. Inca warriors were killed trying to protect their king. The ground ran red with blood. In the end, the Spaniards murdered almost all the guards. They arrested Atahuallpa and placed him in a cell.

Pizarro went to visit his prisoner. He told Atahuallpa,

Do not take it as an insult that you have been defeated and taken prisoner, for with the Christians who come with me, though so few in number, I have conquered greater kingdoms than yours, and have defeated other more powerful lords than you.

Atahuallpa had no way of knowing that Pizarro lied. Had

In his attack on Atahuallpa's forces, Pizarro received a cut on his hand from one of his men's swords. It was the only injury the Spanish forces suffered.

not the Spaniard defeated Atahuallpa's great Inca army? Of course, Pizarro had tricked the Sapa Inca and ambushed a small portion of his army. Furthermore, Pizarro's men had superior weapons. In close combat, Spanish swords quickly overcame Inca slings and clubs.

While his men attacked the Inca soldiers, Pizarro fought his way to the Inca ruler.

Pizarro had won. It was time for gold, at last. 🐍

7 ATAHUALLPA'S RANSOM

⤳⤳⤳

The day after the massacre in Cajamarca, Hernando de Soto and a company of Spaniards rode up to the Inca camp. De Soto found great riches in the camp. He ordered his men to collect as much treasure as they could. According to Pedro Pizarro, de Soto returned to Pizarro with emeralds, gold, and silver "in monstrous effigies, large and small dishes, pitchers, jugs, basins, and large drinking vessels, and various other pieces."

Then, Atahuallpa made a serious error. He claimed that his officers had already taken much more gold, silver, and gems away from the camp. He bragged of his cleverness, and the Spaniards decided to make him pay a ransom for his release.

Atahuallpa was afraid that his brother Huáscar

Inca subjects brought riches from throughout the empire to fill Atahuallpa's ransom room.

Atahuallpa, the Sapa Inca, wore special clothing and jewelry to show his rank. Because the Incas did not have a written language, Atahuallpa's name is often spelled different ways.

ATHABALIBA
ultimus Rex Peruanorum

might escape from his Inca prison and come to power while Atahuallpa was a prisoner, so Atahuallpa agreed to the ransom. According to legend, Pizarro placed a mark on a storeroom wall and asked the Inca ruler to fill the room to the mark with gold, silver, and other items valuable to the Spanish. Atahuallpa then raised the mark. The room measured about 22 feet by 17 feet (6.7 meters by 5.2 meters), and Atahuallpa's mark reached about 8 feet (2.5 m) high.

The Spaniards treated Atahuallpa like an honored guest. They fed him well. They made his stay pleasant, but they did not let him go. The soldiers guarding him became close friends, often sharing meals with Atahuallpa. The Sapa Inca even learned to play dice and chess and enjoyed playing these games with his captors.

While Atahuallpa was imprisoned, the Spanish sent envoys to speak with Huáscar. Huáscar was still in prison following the Inca civil war, and he promised the Spanish great riches if he could be set free. When Atahuallpa heard this, he plotted to end Huáscar's life. He could not risk the Spanish restoring Huáscar to the throne. Atahuallpa sent trusted captains to Huáscar's prison and had his brother killed. Pizarro suspected that Atahuallpa had arranged the murder, but could prove nothing. Atahuallpa claimed that his men had slain Huáscar without consulting him.

During Atahuallpa's imprisonment, why did the Inca army not attack? How could Pizarro, with so few men, hold off so many soldiers? The answer is that in the Inca world, no one acted unless the Sapa Inca gave the order to do so. While imprisoned by the Spanish, Atahuallpa could not give commands. Without their leader, the Inca army became powerless.

67

Soon, hundreds of men and llamas were traveling from the capital at Cuzco to Cajamarca. They carried gold and silver plates, jewelry, statues, and furniture. Pedro Sancho recorded the gold and silver offered as ransom:

> ... *five hundred odd plates of gold from some house walls in Cuzco; and even the smallest plates weighed four or five pounds apiece; other larger ones weighed ten or twelve pounds, and with plates of this sort the walls of the temple were covered. They also brought a seat of very fine gold, worked into the form of a footstool, which weighed eighteen thousand pesos [a Spanish gold weight].*

The Inca subjects found the Spanish desire for gold strange. For them, gold belonged to Inti, their sun god. They believed gold was the sweat of the sun and had no real value. In fact, Inca culture prized well-woven cloth above gold. The Incas joked about the Spaniards' love of gold and silver. Some believed the Spanish actually ate the metal.

With the ransom paid, Atahuallpa expected to be set free. However, Pizarro was no fool. He realized that, once free, Atahuallpa could gather his army. Atahuallpa would never allow the Spanish to leave the Andes with Inca gold. Therefore, Pizarro would never allow Atahuallpa out of jail.

About this time, Almagro and his men arrived, much to the frustration of Pizarro's soldiers. By contract, Almagro's company could demand a share of the treasure. Pizarro's company disagreed with this arrangement. They took all the risks, faced the thousands of Inca soldiers, and came away victorious. They were irritated that Almagro's men expected a share without having done any of the hard work. Pizarro's company further claimed that Atahuallpa's contract for the ransom was made with Pizarro and his men and not with other Spaniards far from Cajamarca. Finally, the matter was decided between Pizarro and Almagro. The latecomers received a small portion of the gold and silver—a very small portion compared to Pizarro and his soldiers.

The Spanish took the Sapa Inca's ransom and melted the gold and silver down into coins and bars. This made it easier to divide the wealth, and easier to ship it back to Spain as well. The Spaniards did not care about the artistry of the jewelry, goblets, and statues. They needed gold and silver to fight wars in Europe.

Inca subjects mined their gold both from rocks as well as by sifting through river gravel for small chunks. Much of the gold that was recovered was sent to Cuzco, the Inca capital, where craftspeople fashioned it into jewelry, plates, statues, or other decorative items. Most items were made by pouring melted gold into a mold and allowing it to cool and harden into the chosen shape.

The Incas created beautiful decorations, like this toucan, out of jewels and precious metals.

It was the quantity of gold, not the artistry of its form, that pleased the Spanish king.

When goldsmiths finished melting the gold and silver into standard Spanish measures, Pizarro divided up the ransom. In all, he had collected about 13,420 pounds (6,039 kg) of gold and 26,000 pounds (11,700 kg) of silver. King Charles V received his "royal fifth" that was sent by ship to Spain. The average cavalry soldier received 8,880 gold pieces and 362 silver marcs. Pizarro received 57,222 pieces of gold and 2,350 marcs of silver. Pizarro also accepted the great gold throne of the Sapa Inca, worth about

25,000 pieces of gold. At today's prices, he was a millionaire many times over. Francisco Pizarro was finally rich.

Now that the Spaniards had divided the ransom, they still faced the problem of what to do with Atahuallpa. Instead of the freedom he expected, Atahuallpa found himself on trial for his life.

Pizarro accused Atahuallpa of ordering his brother's death, killing about 1,000 nobles and commoners, misusing Inca funds, and having more than one wife. In all, Atahuallpa had to answer 12 serious charges.

Atahuallpa stood trial in a court of Spanish law, headed by Almagro and Pizarro as judges. The topic of the ransom was not discussed. Not surprisingly, the court found Atahuallpa guilty. Atahuallpa spoke to Pizarro:

> *What have I done, or my children, that I should meet such a fate? And from your hands, too, you, who have met with friendship and kindness from my people, with whom I have shared my treasures, who have received nothing but benefits from my hands.*

The court sentenced Atahuallpa to death by burning. This horrified the Inca king, who believed in life after death only if his body remained whole.

Because he accepted Christianity before his death, Pizarro's men strangled Atahuallpa instead of burning him.

On August 29, 1533, Atahuallpa was led to his execution. His hands and feet were chained to prevent his escape. Father Valverde gave Atahuallpa a final chance to accept the Spaniards' one true Christian God. Atahuallpa agreed to become a Catholic if Pizarro's court would strangle him instead of death by fire. Father Valverde baptized the fallen Inca leader as Juan de Atahuallpa. Immediately after the baptism, Atahuallpa was strangled to death.

With the death of Atahuallpa, Pizarro believed he had defeated the Incas. The vast riches of the Inca empire were now his for the taking. Inca chronicler Garcilaso de la Vega wrote,

> *Once the two kings, Huáscar Inca and Atahuallpa, who were brothers as well as enemies, were dead, the Spaniards remained supreme masters of both Peruvian kingdoms [Cuzco and Quito], there being no one left to oppose or even contradict them ... all the Indians ... had remained after their kings were gone, like sheep without a shepherd.*

A small troop of Spaniards had conquered an empire of millions with very little effort. But many troubles lay ahead for Pizarro and his men, and some of them were to come from the Spanish themselves. ✍

8 TROUBLES IN CUZCO

ೕೲ

After the death of Atahuallpa, Pizarro, Almagro, and their men marched to Cuzco, the Inca capital. They were in a hurry in case there was any more gold left in the capital after the payment of Atahuallpa's ransom. They couldn't risk anyone else getting any gold they could claim for themselves.

Cuzco was at 11,000 feet (3,353 meters) above sea level on a high plain between mountain peaks. Cuzco was designed in the shape of a puma, an animal revered by the Incas for its cunning and strength. At the puma's head stood Sacsahuaman, a stone fortress. The fortress was built in the shape of a puma's teeth. In the puma's midsection, the Incas had arranged palaces, temples, and a school around a broad plaza. The Coricancha, the Inca's temple to

Pizarro's brother Juan died fighting the Incas at the fortress of Sacsahuaman in Cuzco.

In the Incan language, Quechua, Cuzco means "navel of the world."

their sun god, stood in a place of honor on the plaza. Nearby, a large group of holy women lived in the conventlike Acllahuasi. The homes of noble families were in the tail of the puma, where two river canals joined together.

Cuzco's residents welcomed Pizarro and Almagro. They had not liked Atahuallpa and were glad to learn of his death. In addition, Pizarro wisely named another one of Atahuallpa's brothers, Manco Inca, as the new Sapa Inca. Few people realized that Manco Inca would serve as a puppet ruler with no power. Still, he was a son of the great leader Huayna Capac, and the people welcomed his leadership.

In Cuzco, the Spanish found packed warehouses filled with dried potatoes and meat, bolts of fine cloth, tools, and weapons. Pizarro's cousin Pedro claimed,

> *There were so many warehouses of wonderful textiles ... of gilded thrones, of food, of coca leaves ... clothes made of sewn sequins of very delicate and exquisite workmanship ... storehouses of copper tools ... cups and plates in silver ... twelve llamas of silver and gold, lifelike and life size.*

Pizarro, Almagro, and their troops went through Cuzco and gathered up every valuable item in sight. They emptied the storehouses. The Spanish showed no respect for the Inca religion. They robbed and sacked the Coricancha, the Incas' holy temple.

About this time, Pizarro took an Inca princess as his common-law wife. Although they did not marry, Pizarro called her his wife and introduced her as such. Originally named Quispe Cusi, Pizarro's Inca wife took the name Inés Yupanqui. Pizarro nicknamed her Pizpita, after a bird from his native Spain.

In 1534, Inés gave birth to a daughter, Francisca. A year later was the birth of a son, named Gonzalo after Pizarro's father. Pizarro would later ask the Spanish courts to recognize them as his legal heirs. Pizarro also fathered two other sons, Juan and Francisco, by another Inca woman—Angelina Añas

Yupanqui. Juan and Francisco never became Pizarro's legal heirs.

Pizarro did not want Cuzco as his capital. He needed a port city from which he could ship gold to Spain. In 1535, Pizarro founded the *Ciudad de los Reyes*, or City of Kings. This city became Lima, the capital of present-day Peru. The city lay at the mouth of the Rimac River. Its layout was simple: 13 streets by nine, or 117 city blocks. The streets were so straight that a person standing at any intersection could see clearly past the city's limits in every direction. Pizarro ordered churches, homes, and palaces built in the Spanish style. One hundred of Pizarro's men moved into his new capital.

Back in Spain, gold and silver arrived from Peru. King Charles V was thrilled. Royalty always needed money. He rewarded Pizarro and Almagro, making them governors over a divided Inca empire. Pizarro got the northern half, and Almagro received the southern part. Cuzco fell in Almagro's region, which upset the Pizarro brothers. They believed Francisco should have received everything valuable in Peru. They had fought beside their half brother and resented Almagro getting anything.

When the news of their reward reached Peru, Almagro decided to inspect his newly gained territory. In July 1535, he left to tour his land, part of present-day Chile. He expected to find great riches in his new territory, just as the Spanish had found riches in Peru. He brought more than 200 troops

The cathedral of Lima was built during Pizarro's time.

with him, as well as 12,000 Inca soldiers provided by Manco Inca, the puppet Inca ruler.

As soon as Almagro left Cuzco, Pizarro placed his half brothers Juan and Gonzalo in charge of the city. This was a major mistake. The Spanish craved gold, frequently abused native women, and robbed the Inca people. Juan and Gonzalo proved to be the worst of the lot. They ransacked the Coricancha temple and abused several holy women. Governor Francisco Pizarro knew of his brothers' offenses, yet he did nothing. He was too busy setting up his capital to monitor his brothers' behavior in Cuzco. Besides, Francisco was not much interested in the Inca people—only the Inca gold.

By the end of 1535, the Inca people had suffered under the Pizarro brothers long enough. Their weak leader Manco Inca tried to escape from Cuzco and raise an army. His plans were leaked to the Pizarros, who captured the departing Manco and ordered him put in a dungeon. The Inca subjects could not act without orders from above. With their leader now in jail, the people continued to suffer.

The Inca empire was in a terrible state. For more than 300 years, the people had served their ruler. Inca commoners provided labor to the empire, and the Sapa Inca and priests stored the food, weapons, crafts, and cloth the people made to help support them during hard times. The Spanish were not concerned about the welfare of the natives. They stole, used, and wasted whatever stores existed. When crops failed in 1536, there was no backup food supply. The natives, once protected and fed by their rulers, faced starvation.

Finally, Manco Inca escaped Cuzco and retreated into the Amazon rain forest. He made his base in the small city of Vilcabamba. The Pizarros' repeated efforts to find and recapture Manco Inca failed. By this time, no Inca subject would tell the Spanish anything except under torture. But the Spanish did not hesitate to use torture to get information.

The Spaniards treated the Incas cruelly, often torturing them in order to get information.

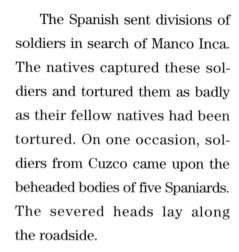

For eight years, Manco Inca continued to fight the Spanish while managing to avoid capture. He moved from one hideout to another. In 1544, however, the Spanish penetrated his fortress at Vilcabamba. There they assassinated him without the show trial and execution Atahuallpa had been given.

The Spanish sent divisions of soldiers in search of Manco Inca. The natives captured these soldiers and tortured them as badly as their fellow natives had been tortured. On one occasion, soldiers from Cuzco came upon the beheaded bodies of five Spaniards. The severed heads lay along the roadside.

Back in Lima, every Spanish ship brought more Spaniards to Peru. The lure of gold drew flocks of men anxious to get rich quickly. Many joined Francisco Pizarro's military. Others realized that their lives depended on a united front against the huge native population. The Spanish would stop at nothing to hold Peru and take advantage of that nation's wealth.

By the time Hernando Pizarro had joined his brothers in Cuzco, clashes between the Spanish and Incas had increased. The Incas set up positions around Cuzco, placing that city under siege. Within the boundaries of Cuzco, little food remained. Hernando fed his own people and let the Incas starve. He led attacks against the Incas, killing many and raiding as much food as possible. The battle reached its climax when the Spaniards attacked the

Incas at the fortress of Sacsahuaman. Many soldiers from both sides were killed in the fighting, including Pizarro's brother Juan. The Spanish eventually captured the fortress and turned it into a prison.

When the Inca soldiers left the fields around Cuzco, Hernando Pizarro sensed victory was his. His men scoured the countryside, stealing llamas, corn, and potatoes. They left little or nothing for natives to eat. They met any protest with guns or swords.

In 1537, Diego de Almagro returned from his trip to Chile thoroughly disgusted. Chile had proved

The Incas and Spanish clashed in Cuzco. Later, the Spanish fought among themselves.

worthless—no gold, no silver, and no gems. Now, Almagro found Cuzco—his king's gift—in dreadful conditions. The siege of Cuzco had killed nearly 20,000 natives. Thousands of other natives were starving. Almagro was enraged and demanded the city be returned to his control. Hernando Pizarro refused.

The boldness and cruelty of the Pizarros angered Almagro. In April 1537, Almagro's company, called the Men of Chile, attacked the Pizarro brothers' quarters in Cuzco. They set the roof on fire and captured Gonzalo and Hernando. Francisco Pizarro sent troops to fight against Almagro's men.

All did not go well with Almagro's recapture of Cuzco. Gonzalo escaped Almagro's jail and quickly headed to Lima to report to his brother. Francisco Pizarro relied on his long-term friendship with Almagro to settle the situation. He promised Almagro that he could keep Cuzco—if Hernando were set free. Foolishly, Almagro believed his former partner.

In April 1538, a major battle raged between Pizarro's men and Almagro's Men of Chile at Las Salinas. Pizarro's men won the fight, which claimed 150 lives. In this battle, Hernando captured Almagro and put him in prison. An endless parade of Almagro's enemies saw a chance to pay Almagro back for past offenses. They lay charges against Almagro, and Hernando Pizarro arranged a trial.

Although the charges were false, the court found Almagro guilty. Hernando ordered his enemy beheaded. However, before this could take place, Diego de Almagro was strangled in his jail cell.

Spaniards quickly took sides over Almagro's unfair trial and murder. Reports sped by ship to King Charles V, telling of the Pizarro brothers' treachery. Almagro had been known as an unpleasant man who bragged too much and lost his temper too often, but he had been loyal to his king and had helped conquer the Inca empire. While it was true that Almagro had his enemies, so did the Pizarros. Almagro, at least, had treated the natives with some level of respect.

Back in Spain, King Charles V burned with anger over the death of Almagro. ❧

In 1539, Hernando Pizarro returned to Spain. To his surprise, Charles V had him jailed for the murder of Diego de Almagro. Hernando protested, appealed, and stalled. He did not wish to give up his lands and riches that had been earned at Almagro's expense. And so, Hernando lingered in jail for many years, although he suffered no hardships. He lived in a series of apartments, had servants, and ate well. He even received visitors.

9 FINAL YEARS

Now, Francisco and his brothers ruled all of the former Inca empire. Francisco doled out land to his friends. The Spanish had put in place a new system, called *encomienda*. This system granted the new Spanish landowners the right to the labor of the natives who lived on the land. They were required to work for him part-time, either on the land itself or in another activity, such as weaving cloth.

Some natives received money for their work. However, the Inca people knew nothing of money. Their culture did not revere gold; it honored hard work. In the past, they had paid taxes with their labor. Now, they were expected to pay money— whatever that was—for their needs.

By the late 1530s, Peru's countryside and native

Supporters of Diego de Almagro were eventually able to take final revenge against Francisco Pizarro.

people had suffered severe hardship. Father Valverde, who had taken part in Atahuallpa's capture, wrote to his king:

> *I moved across a good portion of this land and saw terrible destruction in it. Having seen the land before, I could not help feeling great sadness. The sight of such desolation would move anyone to great pity.*

Francisco Pizarro did not care what happened to Peru's land or people. He was too busy enjoying the wealth he stole and the lifestyle he had yearned for. He had built a luxurious mansion for himself in the heart of Lima. He enjoyed his family. He had servants to cook, clean, and care for his every need. He never went hungry, and he did not care that Peru's people did. In short, he became the wealthiest and, perhaps, the most hated person in Peru.

In contrast, Almagro's followers had little to be happy about now. By Governor Pizarro's order, they had to live in Lima. They were not in prison, but neither were they completely free. Pizarro had

Under Peru's system of encomienda, a conquistador could also ask for tribute, or tax, from the natives. Every year, a landowner was entitled to receive 2,500 pesos de oro, 640 bushels of wheat, 800 bushels of barley, 200 bushels of corn, 30 llamas, and 30 pigs. This left very little for the natives to live on.

By the time he had conquered Cuzco, Pizarro was nearly 70 years old—a very old man in the 16th century.

guards watching the Men of Chile. Their movements and meetings became daily reports to Governor Pizarro. Yet under the watchful eye of Pizarro's troops, the Men of Chile met and planned the governor's assassination. It was scheduled for June 26, 1541, and involved a surprise attack as the governor left church that day.

Word of the attack leaked to the governor. Pizarro, instead of attending Mass in church, stayed home. He planned to deal with the rebels later. The Men of Chile revised their plan. They would assault Pizarro in the governor's mansion.

That Sunday night, Pizarro had invited about 20 guests to dine at his palace in Lima. The guest list included Pizarro's half brother Francisco Martinez de Alcántara, Lima's Judge Velasquez, and a priest who was to become bishop of Quito. The dinner went smoothly, and the guests ate well. They toasted their host with fine Spanish port wine. The guests chatted, laughed, and shared local gossip.

Then Almagro's supporters broke into the governor's palace. Pizarro tried to fight off their attack. According to accounts written at the time, he brandished a sword and dagger against his murderers. He managed to kill three of Almagro's followers, but the attackers cut him many times, and Pizarro bled to death. His half brother, Alcántara, was killed in the struggle. As he lay dying, Pizarro drew a cross on the floor with his own blood. He kissed the cross and cried, "Jesus."

Francisco Pizarro was buried behind the cathedral of Lima. In 1545, his body, minus his skull, was reburied under the main altar. His skull was placed in a lead box with the Spanish words: "Here is the skull of the Marquis Don Francisco Pizarro, who discovered and won Peru and placed it under the crown of Castile."

CAPITAN GENERAL
DON FRANCISCO PIZARRO.

FUNDADOR DE LIMA
EN 18 DE ENERO DE 1535
MUERTO EN 26 DE JUNIO DE 1541.

FUERON DEPOSITADOS SUS RESTOS EN ESTA URNA
EL 28 DE JUNIO E 1891
POR ACUERDO DEL H. CONCEJO PROVINCIAL DE LIMA
Y POR INICIATIVA
DEL SR. ALCALDE D. JUAN REVOREDO

Pizarro is buried in the cathedral of Lima in the city he helped found.

After Pizarro's death, the Spanish king's official forces arrived in Peru to take control. They imposed laws that took away much of Pizarro's former soldiers' wealth. Pizarro's brother Gonzalo, along with other soldiers, fought the king's forces. Gonzalo was executed as a rebel in 1548. With his death, the Pizarro brothers of Peru were all either dead or in prison. ॐ

Chapter 10 PIZARRO'S LEGACY

❦

It is said that the Incas built a magnificent empire in 400 years, and the Spanish destroyed it in less than four years. Pizarro and his company showed no respect for Inca customs or the Inca people. Gold fever burned too brightly in their eyes for them to see anything but riches for the taking.

The Roman Catholic Church insisted that all natives become Catholic. Priests destroyed Inca idols and places of worship. They built Catholic churches on top of ruined Inca temples. Holy places and shrines, or *huacas*, were destroyed; priests replaced idols with rosary beads. The Spanish banned all Inca festivals. They substituted planting and harvest rites with Catholic holy days and saints' days. Priests baptized Inca natives as Catholics,

The Spaniards never found the Inca city of Machu Picchu. As a result, historians were able to study its remains to learn more about life in the Inca empire.

Catholicism long ago replaced the traditional Inca religion. Still, Cuzco honors its Inca past by holding the ceremony of Inti Raymi—the winter solstice— each June.

whether the natives wanted to be Catholic or not. Today, nine out of 10 people living in the former Inca empire follow the Roman Catholic religion.

The Incas also had to learn Spanish. Countries that Pizarro once ruled with an iron fist continue to use Spanish as their main language. Yet, even as Spanish became the dominant language, many natives kept their Inca language and Inca customs. Natives spoke Spanish in public, and Quechua, the Inca language, at home. Some dared to hold Inca religious events in secret. Creation tales and legends of Inca history became whispers in the night. That was the only way to save their Inca heritage. In Peru, Quechua survives as the "second" official language.

Pizarro and his company are long gone from Peru. Yet the sound of their voices is heard in the Spanish spoken on every street. Spanish culture thrives in Peru's music, food, and art.

Many Peruvian cities still bear Inca names— for example, Tumbes, Cuzco, and Huancayo. And although palaces and churches through- out Peru show Spanish influence, many were built on top of Inca foundation stones.

Although it may be conflicted and painful, this legacy is testament to the remarkable accomplishments of Francisco Pizarro. A soldier with no formal schooling and who could neither read nor write, Pizarro transformed the history of Peru. He was driven to achieve wealth for himself and his country. Despite great odds, he headed an expedition that explored a brand-new world and that ultimately brought a vast and populous empire to an end.

PIZARRO'S LIFE

BETWEEN 1471 AND 1475

Born in Trujillo, Spain

1502

Sails to Hispaniola with the new governor

1470

1500

1474

Isabella becomes queen of Aragon and known as the "First Lady of the Renaissance"

1492

Ferdinand and Isabella of Spain finance the voyage of the Italian Christopher Columbus to the New World

WORLD EVENTS

1513

Takes part in expedition that reaches the Pacific Ocean

1522

Joins failed Andagoya expedition to the South

1509

Joins expedition with Alonso de Ojeda

1520

1509

Henry, Prince of Wales, at age 18, becomes King Henry VIII of England

1517

Martin Luther posts his 95 theses on the door of the Palast Church in Wittenberg, beginning the Protestant Reformation in Germany

PIZARRO'S LIFE

1524

Sets sail for Birú
(Peru) along the
Pacific Coast

1525

Signs a contract
forming a partnership
with Almagro

1525

1524

German peasants rise
up against their land-
lords in The Peasant's
War, the greatest
mass uprising in
German history

WORLD EVENTS

1530

Receives royal permission to begin conquest of Peru

1532

Holds Atahuallpa for ransom

1528

Arrives in Tumbes, Peru

1530

1531

The "great comet," later called Halley's Comet, causes a wave of superstition

1529

The pope refuses to grant England's King Henry VIII a divorce, setting the stage for England's separation from the Roman Catholic Church

PIZARRO'S LIFE

1535

Founds the city of
Lima, Peru; with
brothers, takes
over Cuzco

1533

Atahuallpa is executed
after a Spanish-style
trial; Manco Inca is
crowned Sapa Inca

1535

1535

The first complete
English translation
of the Bible is printed
in Germany

1534

French explorer
Jacques Cartier enters
the St. Lawrence
River and establishes
French presence in
Canada

WORLD EVENTS

1538

A power struggle sets Pizarro and Almagro at war with each other; Hernando Pizarro arranges Almagro's assassination

1536-1537

Inca subjects revolt against Spanish rule

1541

Killed in Lima, Peru, by supporters of Almagro

1540

1540

Spanish explorer Francisco Vasquez de Coronado leads an expedition into what is now the southwestern United States

DATE OF BIRTH: Unknown date, probably between 1471 and 1475

BIRTHPLACE: Trujillo, Spain

FATHER: Gonzalo Pizarro

MOTHER: Francisca Gonzalez

EDUCATION: None, could not read or write

SPOUSE: Inés Haylas Yupanqui (common-law)

DATE OF MARRIAGE: None

CHILDREN: Francisca, Gonzalo, Juan, Francisco

DATE OF DEATH: July 26, 1541

PLACE OF BURIAL: Lima, Peru

In the Library

Bernand, Carmen. *The Incas: People of the Sun.* New York: Harry N. Abrams, Inc., 1993.

De Angelis, Gina. *Francisco Pizarro and the Conquest of the Inca.* Broomall, Pa.: Chelsea House Publishing, 2000.

Ingram, Scott. *Francisco Pizarro. History's Villains.* San Diego: Blackbirch, 2002.

Lourie, Peter. *Lost Treasure of the Inca.* Honesdale, Pa.: Boyds Mills Press, 1999.

ON THE WEB

For more information on *Francisco Pizarro*, use FactHound to track down Web sites related to this book.

1. Go to *www.facthound.com*
2. Type in a search word related to this book or this book ID: 0756508150
3. Click on the *Fetch It* button.

FactHound will find the best Web sites for you.

HISTORIC SITES

American Museum of Natural History
Central Park West at 79th Street
New York, NY 10024-5192
212/769-5100
To see exhibits on the art, architecture, and customs of the Incas

The Mariners' Museum
100 Museum Drive
Newport News, VA 23606
757/596-2222
To see exhibits about navigators, their ships, and other maritime artifacts

assassination
a murder, usually for political reasons

chain mail
a garment made of linked metal chains used to protect the wearer during battle

chronicler
a person who writes the history of a culture or nation

coat of arms
a group of designs that make up a special sign of a person or family; only knights, nobles, or the very wealthy were allowed to have coats of arms.

colony
a territory settled by people from another country and controlled by that country

common-law
an unofficial relationship, usually a marriage

conquistador
a Spanish conqueror, such as Pizarro or Cortés

doctrines
the beliefs of a group of people

doublet
a close-fitting jacket worn by European men between the 15th and 17th centuries

expedition
a long journey taken for a special purpose; the group of people making the journey

interpreters
a person who explains what someone else said in a different language

legacy
something handed down by custom or tradition

litter
a platform used to carry a single person

medieval
of or relating to the Middle Ages, from 400 to 1500

mortar
a building material used to hold stones or bricks together

musket
an early gun with a long barrel

mutiny
an open revolt against a person or persons in authority

royal fifth
the portion of the treasure taken in an expedition or conquest—one-fifth—that was paid to the king in tribute

smallpox
a deadly disease common in the 1500s and 1600s

solstice
in winter, the shortest day of the year; in summer, the longest day of the year

treason
the act of betraying one's country by helping an enemy

vassal
a loyal follower of a nobleman

Chapter 3

Page 26, line 9: Albert Marrin. *Inca and Spaniard: Pizarro and the Conquest of Peru.* New York: Macmillan Publishing Company, 1989, p. 56.

Page 29, line 5: Bruce Ruiz. "Balboa—His Execution." www.bruce.ruiz.net/PanamaHistory/vasco_nunez_balboa_6.htm.

Page 29, line 16: Ibid.

Chapter 4

Page 42, line 15: Michael Wood. *Conquistadors.* Los Angeles: University of California Press, 2000, p. 120.

Page 43, line 1: William H. Prescott. *History of the Conquest of Mexico and History of the Conquest of Peru.* New York: Random House, 1989, p. 263.

Chapter 5

Page 50, line 6: Chasqui Amaru. *Inca Prophecies.* www.pacaritambo.com/cuzco.html

Page 55, line 25: Fred Ramen. *Francisco Pizarro: The Exploration of Peru and the Conquest of the Inca.* New York: Rosen Publishing, 2004, p. 7.

Chapter 6

Page 60, line 24: Carmen Bernand. *The Incas: People of the Sun.* New York: Harry N. Abrams, Inc., 1993, p. 131.

Page 62, line 18: Ibid., p. 133.

Chapter 7

Page 65, line 7: John Hemming. *The Conquest of the Incas.* London: Papermac, 1993, p. 48.

Page 68, line 6: *Inca and Spaniard: Pizarro and the Conquest of Peru,* p. 115. Title, p. 115.

Page 71, line 18: *History of the Conquest of Mexico and History of the Conquest of Peru,* ch. 7.

Page 73, line 5: Garcilaso de la Vega. *The Incas: The Royal Commentaries of the Inca Garcilaso de la Vega. Book 10.* (Trans. Alain Gheerbrant). New York: The Orion Press, 1961, p. 365.

Chapter 8

Page 77, line 4: *Conquistadors,* p. 148.

Chapter 9

Page 88, line 4: Lee Klein. "Francisco Pizarro—A Head of his Time." *The California Native International Adventures.* www.calnative.com/stories/n_pizarro.htm.

Select Bibliography

Bernand, Carmen. *The Incas: People of the Sun.* New York: Harry N. Abrams, Inc., 1993.

Cieza de León, Pedro de. *Chronicle of Peru.* (Second Part). Trans. Clements R. Markham. London: Hakluyt Society, 1883.

Cobo, Father Bernabé. *The History of the New World.* Obtained on microfiche by the public library.

Hemming, John. *The Conquest of the Incas.* London: Papermac, 1993.

Marrin, Albert. *Inca and Spaniard: Pizarro and the Conquest of Peru.* New York: Macmillan Publishing Company, 1989.

Pizarro, Pedro. *Relation of the Discovery and Conquest of the Kingdoms of Peru.* Trans. Philip Ainsworth Means. New York: Cortes Society, 1921.

Prescott, William H. *History of the Conquest of Mexico and History of the Conquest of Peru.* New York: Random House, 1989.

Ramen, Fred. *Francisco Pizarro: The Exploration of Peru and the Conquest of the Inca.* New York: Rosen Publishing, 2004.

Vega, Garcilaso de la. *The Incas: The Royal Commentaries of the Inca Garcilaso de la Vega.* Trans. Alain Gheerbrant. New York: The Orion Press, 1961.

Wood, Michael. *Conquistadors.* Los Angeles: University of California Press, 2000.

Barbara A. Somervill has been writing for more than 30 years. She has written newspaper and magazine articles, video scripts, and books for children. She enjoys writing about science and investigating people's lives for biographies. She is an avid reader and traveler. Ms. Somervill lives with her husband in South Carolina.

Image Credits